I0454355

The Journey Within

"Where, Why, What" Series

The Dedication

This book is dedicated to the people who believe in the impossible. It's dedicated to those who understand that adversity and obstacles are part of the journey. To those who recognize that, in the micro, the hills along with the valleys are actually, in the macro, steps to the next level. Cheers to the believers who are stubborn enough to keep pushing towards their dreams. Thank you for being an inspiration for others even in the midst of the ups and downs through your journey.

Chapter 1: The Janitor's Discovery

Ray had been a janitor for the same cleaning company for years. His days were mundane, filled with the repetitive routine of tidying up the offices and emptying trash bins. But in the midst of his seemingly monotonous work, Ray found solace in daydreaming about a different life, a life with purpose and direction.

One fateful night, while cleaning the building as usual, Ray stumbled upon something extraordinary. As he opened the janitor's closet door, he felt an unusual sensation, as if an invisible force was drawing him inside. Intrigued, he cautiously stepped into the closet, and to his astonishment, found himself transported to a mysterious and enchanting land – the Land of "Where."

In this mystical realm, Ray encountered the Guardian of Where, an ethereal being with wisdom beyond comprehension.

The Guardian welcomed him warmly and explained that the Land of Where was a place of profound significance, where the power to shape destinies lay. Ray was captivated by this revelation and wanted to know more.

Over time, as Ray continued his nightly cleaning routine, he embraced the Land of Where as his secret sanctuary. Each time he entered the janitor's closet, he embarked on a profound journey that transcended the boundaries of time. For every second spent in the Land of Where, Ray experienced the passage of days.

Now, Ray had been a janitor at the office building for years. Each night, he diligently cleaned the premises, making sure everything was spotless by the time the sun rose. The office was typically empty during his shift, except for one late-night worker named Joseph.

Joseph, an enigmatic man, seemed to be consumed by his work. Ray would often catch glimpses of him working late into the evening, lost in his own world of paperwork and charts. Their encounters were brief and in passing, but Ray couldn't help but be intrigued by the mysterious man.

One night, fueled by his excitement about the time he had been spending in the Land of Where, Ray decided to break the silence and introduce himself to Joseph. He approached Joseph cautiously, initiating a conversation.

As they exchanged pleasantries, Ray couldn't resist asking about the Land of Where, hoping to find a kindred spirit who had also experienced its wonders.

However, Joseph's response caught Ray off guard. The typically reserved man gave him an interesting look, one that seemed to suggest a mixture of surprise and disbelief. Ray quickly changed the subject, not wanting to appear like a lunatic for bringing up such a peculiar topic.

Puzzled by Joseph's reaction, Ray couldn't shake off the feeling that something was amiss. He knew Joseph had been working at the office for a long time and must have been in the janitor's closet before. Yet, Joseph's response seemed to imply that he had no knowledge of the Land of Where's existence.

Determined to unravel the mystery, Ray decided to bide his time before bringing up the subject again. He continued his nightly routine, secretly visiting the Land of Where whenever he had a chance. In the quiet solitude of the Land of Where, Ray found solace and gained wisdom from his conversations with the Guardian of Where.

Weeks passed, and Ray couldn't stop pondering over Joseph's odd reaction. Despite his curiosity, he chose to remain patient, waiting for the right moment to revisit the topic.

The Land of Where became a sanctuary, a place where Ray could escape the mundane reality of his daily life as a janitor, even if only for a fleeting moment.

As he continued his nighttime visits to the Land of Where, Ray started to notice changes in himself. His goals became clearer, his aspirations more defined. The wisdom he gained from the Guardian of Where began to shape his perspective on life and his purpose. Deep within, Ray felt a newfound sense of purpose and determination.

Little did he know that his encounters with the Keeper of How and the Taker of When were just around the corner, waiting to challenge him and test his resolve on his journey to becoming the best version of himself.

The Keepers of How and Takers of When had their own motives, lurking in the shadows, trying to prevent Ray from unlocking the true potential of his "Where."

But Ray was determined to stay true to the path he had discovered and embrace the guidance of the Guardian of Where, for he knew that in the Land of Where, lay the key to his future self.

Chapter 2: The Enigmatic Joseph

In the following days, Ray couldn't shake off the lingering curiosity about Joseph's peculiar response to his inquiry about the Land of Where. He pondered over the possibilities, wondering if Joseph was simply playing coy or if there was more to the story. Each night as he cleaned the offices, he stole glances at Joseph, trying to decipher any clues that might shed light on the mystery.

One evening, as the clock struck midnight, Ray noticed Joseph engrossed in his work as usual. With a deep breath, he decided to approach him again, determined to get some answers.
As he neared Joseph's desk, he noticed intricate diagrams and calculations spread across the surface.

"Hey, Joseph," Ray spoke with a hint of nervousness in his voice.

Joseph looked up, his eyes betraying a momentary surprise before settling back into his composed demeanor. "Hello, Ray. What can I help you with?"

Summoning his courage, Ray decided to be direct. "I hope you don't mind me asking, but the other night, when I mentioned the Land of Where, you seemed surprised. Have you ever been there?"

Joseph's expression remained enigmatic, and he took a moment before responding. "The Land of Where, you say? That's an interesting concept, Ray. Care to enlighten me?"

Ray's heart sank, realizing that Joseph was maintaining his enigmatic facade. "Oh, it's nothing, really. Just something I heard about. Must have been my imagination."

Joseph's lips curled into a faint smile. "Imagination can be a powerful thing, Ray. It's what keeps us curious and exploring the unknown. But sometimes, it's best to focus on the here and now."

Ray felt a pang of disappointment, but he couldn't ignore the spark of intrigue in Joseph's eyes. There was something more to Joseph's cryptic words, and Ray was determined to uncover the truth.

Over the next few weeks, Ray observed Joseph closely, looking for any clues that might lead him to understand the mysteries surrounding the Land of Where. He noticed that Joseph was highly skilled at decoding complex data and had an uncanny ability to predict trends in the market.

One night, as Ray ventured into the Land of Where, he asked the Guardian about Joseph. "Guardian, have you ever encountered someone like Joseph in this realm?"

The Guardian, a radiant being with boundless wisdom, nodded thoughtfully. "Ah, young Ray, the enigmatic ones are not uncommon. They often possess knowledge beyond the ordinary, and their perspectives are shaped by experiences we cannot fathom. The path to their true selves is veiled, and only time will reveal their purpose."

Ray absorbed the Guardian's words, feeling a mix of confusion and determination. He couldn't help but wonder if Joseph's mysterious nature was somehow connected to the Land of Where. Perhaps Joseph held the key to understanding the realm's significance.

As Ray continued to delve into the Land of Where, he found himself facing challenges and obstacles that tested his determination. The Keeper of How and the Taker of When seemed to grow more relentless, attempting to deter him from embracing the wisdom of the Guardian.

Through it all, Ray held on to his vision of a better life, guided by the lessons from the Land of Where. He sought refuge in its mystical presence, finding the courage to face the uncertainties in his own world. The journey to becoming the best version of himself had just begun, and Ray was prepared to navigate the enigmatic paths that lay ahead.

With each night's visit to the Land of Where, he felt a newfound strength and clarity, ready to embrace the challenges and mysteries of his destiny.

Chapter 3: The Guardian's Guidance

As Ray's visits to the Land of Where continued, he found himself drawn to James, a prominent community leader who believed in empowering young aspiring entrepreneurs to achieve their goals. James had a reputation for being a visionary and a guiding light for those seeking success in their ventures. He generously shared his knowledge and experience, offering mentorship to anyone who showed a genuine commitment to their dreams.

One evening, after a particularly enlightening visit to the Land of Where, Ray attended a community event where James was giving a motivational talk. As James spoke about the power of perseverance and the importance of giving back to the community, Ray felt an instant connection to the words spoken. It was as if the wisdom of the Land of Where had materialized before him in human form.

After the talk, Ray mustered the courage to approach James. He introduced himself and expressed his admiration for James' work in the community. As they spoke, Ray couldn't help but notice the genuine warmth and sincerity in James' eyes. He felt an instant bond with the community leader, sensing that he had found another mentor on his journey toward his "Where."

In the following weeks, Ray and James developed a deep connection. James recognized Ray's potential and was eager to guide him on his path to success. He shared his own experiences as an entrepreneur and investor, emphasizing the importance of patience and commitment to the long game.

Ray eagerly absorbed every word, realizing that his trips to the Land of Where were helping him see his true passion as an entrepreneur and investor. The wisdom of the Guardian of Where and the guidance of James were converging, illuminating a clear path toward his "Where."

With newfound determination, Ray embraced the teachings from both realms. He immersed himself in the world of entrepreneurship, attending workshops, networking events, and seeking advice from experienced professionals. Each night, after his visits to the Land of Where, he would reflect on the Guardian's guidance and James' mentorship, drawing strength and inspiration from their wisdom.

As the days turned into months, Ray's transformation became evident to those around him. He exuded a sense of purpose and clarity that attracted like-minded individuals to his side. Through his interactions with aspiring entrepreneurs, Ray became a source of encouragement and motivation, just as the Land of Where and James had been for him.

Joseph, too, remained an integral part of Ray's journey. As a trusted friend, he provided unwavering support and a listening ear. While Joseph didn't fully grasp the wonders of the Land of Where, he understood the profound impact it had on Ray's life and respected his friend's newfound sense of purpose.

As Ray delved deeper into the realms of entrepreneurship and investment, he encountered challenges and setbacks. However, armed with the wisdom of the Land of Where and the mentorship of James, he navigated through obstacles with resilience and determination.

Ray's entrepreneurial endeavors began to flourish, and his investments yielded promising results. He recognized that success wasn't about instant gratification but rather about embracing the long game, planting seeds of growth and patiently nurturing them to fruition.

The Land of Where had shown him that dreams could be achieved through persistence and a clear vision. James had reaffirmed these teachings, guiding him on the path of entrepreneurship with compassion and expertise.

In the midst of his success, Ray never forgot the Guardian of Where and the enigmatic beings that guarded the realm. He continued to visit the Land of Where, seeking counsel and drawing strength from the mystical place that had sparked his transformation.

As Ray's journey continued, he knew that the Land of Where, James, and Joseph would always hold a special place in his heart. Their roles in his life were integral to his growth and success, reminding him that the pursuit of his "Where" was not just a destination but a lifelong commitment to becoming the best version of himself.

Chapter 4: Unraveling the Mystery

As days turned into weeks, Ray's encounters with the Land of Where and the Guardian had become an integral part of his life. Each night, he eagerly looked forward to the moments of solitude in the janitor's closet, where he could transcend the ordinary and venture into the extraordinary realm of possibilities.

During one of his visits to the Land of Where, Ray opened up to the Guardian about his confusion over Joseph's enigmatic response. The Guardian listened attentively, and with a gentle smile, offered mystic secrets that would change Ray's perspective forever.

"Ray," the Guardian began, "the Land of Where holds ancient wisdom that has been passed down through the ages. Among its mystic secrets are visualization techniques and positive affirmations, powerful tools that can unlock the vast potential of your mind."

Puzzled, Ray questioned further, "Visualization and affirmations? How can they help me in my journey?"

The Guardian's serene voice resonated, "Visualization allows you to see your desires clearly and vividly in your mind's eye. By visualizing your goals and aspirations, you create a blueprint for your subconscious mind to follow. As you dwell in these visualizations, your mind begins to believe in the reality of your dreams, making them more attainable."

He continued, "Positive affirmations are like seeds of empowerment planted in the garden of your mind. By repeating affirmations that reinforce your belief in your abilities and your commitment to your goals, you cultivate a mindset of confidence and determination. These affirmations take root in your subconscious, guiding your thoughts and actions towards success."

Ray was captivated by the wisdom the Guardian shared. He felt a deep resonance with the mystical teachings of the Land of Where and realized that these secrets held the key to unlocking his true potential.

A few days later, as he continued his routine, Ray's friend James, the community leader and mentor to young entrepreneurs, approached him with a warm smile. James had noticed a change in Ray's demeanor lately and sensed that something remarkable was happening in his life.

"Ray, my friend," James said, "I've noticed you've been looking rather inspired lately. Care to share what's been going on?"

With newfound confidence, Ray opened up to James about the Land of Where, its mystical secrets, and the profound revelations he had experienced. He spoke about his desires and aspirations to become an entrepreneur and investor and how these mystic secrets of visualization and affirmations had ignited a fire within him.

James listened intently, nodding in understanding. "Ray, you have stumbled upon something extraordinary," he said. "The Land of Where has bestowed upon you ancient wisdom that can shape your destiny. Embrace these visualization techniques and positive affirmations, for they hold the power to unlock your true potential."

But James didn't stop there. He shared stories of successful entrepreneurs who had harnessed the power of visualization and affirmations to manifest their dreams. These anecdotes served as a testament to the effectiveness of the mystic secrets Ray now held.

With newfound determination and armed with the Guardian's wisdom and James's guidance, Ray embarked on his journey toward greatness. The road ahead was filled with uncertainties and surprises, but Ray was now equipped with the knowledge and conviction that he could overcome any obstacle and seize the opportunities that lay ahead.

Chapter 5: The Power of Emotions

In the Land of Where, Ray continued his enlightening conversations with the Guardian, who revealed mystic secrets about the significance of emotions in shaping one's reality. The Guardian emphasized that emotions were not mere fleeting feelings but powerful forces that could influence the course of one's life.

As Ray delved deeper into the topic, he learned that emotions were like energy in motion, as the Latin word "emotere" suggested. The energy generated by emotions could fuel his actions and propel him toward his desired future. The Guardian guided Ray in understanding and channeling his emotions effectively to manifest his aspirations.

Embracing the emotional connection was a transformative experience for Ray. He had always been taught to suppress negative emotions and focus solely on positivity, but the Guardian's teachings were different.

Ray learned that both
positive and negative emotions were
valuable tools on his journey.

Positive emotions fueled his passion,
determination, and sense of purpose.
They provided him with the motivation to
take action and keep moving toward his
"Where." On the other hand, negative
emotions, such as fear and doubt, were
not to be avoided but acknowledged
and understood.

Ray began to understand that emotional
control was essential on his journey to
becoming a successful entrepreneur and
investor. The emotional connection
allowed him to find harmony within
himself. He acknowledged that moments
of doubt or fear were natural but not a
hindrance to his journey. Instead, he saw
them as opportunities for introspection
and growth.

This emotional resilience became a powerful asset as he faced tests of his resolve from the Keeper of How and the Taker of When. These characters continued their efforts to challenge Ray's commitment to the Land of Where's teachings.

The Keeper of How posed questions that made Ray question his path and approach to success. Meanwhile, the Taker of When presented temptations for instant gratification, urging Ray to abandon his long-term vision.

However, Ray's newfound emotional connection was his armor against these tests. He embraced the positive emotions of determination and perseverance to counter impatience. When faced with doubt or uncertainty, he turned to self-compassion, understanding that these emotions were part of the human experience and didn't define his worth or potential.

The Guardian's guidance and Ray's emotional growth complemented each other perfectly. Ray understood that his emotions were not to be suppressed but harnessed for personal transformation. This realization, coupled with his commitment to the long game, allowed him to face these challenges with a sense of purpose and resolve.

As Ray returned from the Land of Where each night, he carried the wisdom of emotional connection with him. It wasn't just about visualizing success or repeating positive affirmations; it was about acknowledging the full spectrum of emotions and using them as catalysts for growth and achievement.

With emotional control as a cornerstone of his journey, Ray was more determined than ever to stay true to his vision and embrace the journey ahead, no matter how challenging it might be.

He understood that the Keeper of How and the Taker of When were not adversaries but characters whose purpose was to test his resolve and determination on his path as an entrepreneur and investor.

Chapter 6: The Quantum Mentorship

As Ray delved deeper into the Land of Where and immersed himself in the mystic secrets of visualization and affirmations, he began to experience a profound transformation within. The Guardian of Where, with its wisdom transcending time, guided him on understanding the power of emotions and how they shape one's reality.

Ray learned that emotional connection was not just a fleeting feeling but a potent force that could mold his future. The Guardian taught him that emotions were like the paintbrush of creation, allowing him to color his life with the hues of his desires and dreams. It was a revelation that resonated deep within Ray's soul, igniting a fire of determination and commitment to his goals.

As Ray continued his nightly visits to the Land of Where, he started to face more tests from the Keeper of How and the Taker of When. These enigmatic characters seemed less like adversaries and more like mentors whose sole purpose was to test his resolve on his journey to becoming the best version of himself.

They challenged him with obstacles and setbacks, knowing that emotional control was paramount on his path to success. Ray realized that his ability to navigate through challenges with grace and poise would determine the trajectory of his future. The Land of Where became a sanctuary for him to hone his emotional resilience and fortitude.

In the midst of these trials, Ray sought guidance from his mentor, James, the community leader who believed in empowering young aspiring entrepreneurs. James had become not only a mentor but also a confidant and a pillar of support for Ray.

One evening, as they sat in James' office, sipping tea and discussing the journey of entrepreneurship, Ray couldn't help but ask about the mystic concept of "the future you" that the Guardian had mentioned. James smiled warmly and explained the concept in a way that left Ray in awe.

"The future you is like a trailblazer," James began, his eyes sparkling with wisdom. "As you walk your path forward, leaving footprints on your journey, the future you is simultaneously leaving breadcrumbs for you to follow. These breadcrumbs serve as messages from your future self, guiding you towards your desired destination."

Ray's mind was buzzing with curiosity and excitement. "So, you mean to say that my future self is helping me navigate through life even before I get there?" he asked, trying to wrap his head around the concept.

"Yes, exactly!" James nodded. "It's like quantum retro causation, where the future influences the present. Your future self is whispering hints and insights into your present, helping you make the right choices and decisions. By connecting with your emotions and your future self's breadcrumbs, you gain the power to shape your own reality."

As Ray absorbed the profound wisdom of quantum retro causation, he felt a deeper sense of unity with his future self. He understood that every step he took, every challenge he faced, and every emotion he experienced were interconnected on the tapestry of his journey.

With newfound clarity and a deeper bond with his future self, Ray continued to apply the wisdom from the Land of Where, the mystic secrets of visualization and affirmations, and the guidance from his mentor, James. He embraced the concept of "the future you" as a guiding light on his entrepreneurial path.

The combination of emotional control, a clear vision of his "where," and the breadcrumbs from his future self allowed Ray to approach his entrepreneurial endeavors with patience and a commitment to the long game. He understood that success was not an overnight phenomenon but a journey paved with determination and dedication.

Ray's journey had become a testament to the power of emotional connection and the profound concept of "the future you." With each passing night in the Land of Where, he drew closer to the future he envisioned, guided not only by the wisdom of the Guardian but also by the empowering mentorship of James.

Chapter 7: The Power of Audacious Dreams

In the Land of Where, Ray's encounters with the Guardian were always filled with wisdom and inspiration. One evening, as they sat under the shimmering glow of celestial lights, the Guardian encouraged Ray to think bigger, to set audacious goals that stretched far beyond his comfort zone.

"Your journey to your 'where' begins with your imagination," the Guardian said, his voice carrying an otherworldly resonance. "Imagine the grandest future you can conceive, for in the realm of dreams, there are no limits."

However, Ray's heart was not immune to self-doubt. The words of the Keepers of How and the Takers of When echoed in his mind, discouraging him from dreaming bigger. They whispered doubts and fears, attempting to hold him back from reaching for greatness.

"Can you truly achieve such grandeur?" the voices taunted. "Why venture into the unknown when you can stay safe within the confines of your comfort zone?"

The battle between Ray's self-doubt and the Guardian's wisdom raged on within him. Yet, with each visit to the Land of Where, he found the courage to confront his fears and insecurities. Slowly but steadily, Ray began to embrace the idea that he was capable of achieving greatness.

Visualizing a grand future became a daily practice for Ray. In the stillness of the Land of Where, he saw himself as a successful entrepreneur and investor, leaving an indelible mark on the world. He imagined his projects coming to life, impacting countless lives, and creating a lasting legacy.

The more Ray visualized his audacious dreams, the more vivid they became. He felt a surge of confidence and determination coursing through him. The self-doubt that once held him captive began to fade, replaced by a newfound belief in his own abilities.

With the Guardian's guidance, Ray learned that the power of audacious dreams lay not just in their grandiosity but in their ability to stretch his potential. He understood that reaching for the stars would require him to grow and evolve as a person.

As Ray continued his visits to the Land of Where, he found himself stepping boldly outside of his comfort zone. He took calculated risks, unafraid of failure, for he knew that every step was a stepping stone toward his grand vision.

The Keepers of How and the Takers of When still lurked in the shadows, but Ray was no longer swayed by their discouraging whispers. He had discovered the strength to silence their influence with his audacious dreams.

Each night, as he left the Land of Where and returned to the real world, Ray carried with him the unyielding belief that he was destined for greatness. The journey ahead was daunting, but he was now armed with audacity and unwavering determination.

With his heart ablaze with purpose and possibility, Ray knew that he was on the cusp of something extraordinary. The Land of Where had shown him the path, and he was ready to walk it, fearlessly pursuing the audacious dreams that would define his destiny.

Chapter 8: Embracing the Long Game

As Ray delved deeper into the Land of Where, he faced a new set of challenges presented by the Taker of When. This elusive figure tempted Ray with alluring shortcuts and immediate gains, attempting to lure him away from his long-term vision. The Taker of When whispered promises of quick success, tempting Ray to abandon his patient approach to entrepreneurship and investing.

At first, the alluring shortcuts seemed enticing to Ray. The idea of achieving rapid results was seductive, and doubt crept into his mind about the long and arduous journey he had embarked upon. But as he reflected on the wisdom of the Guardian and the guidance of James, he recognized the deceptive allure of quick fixes. He understood that lasting success was not built on hasty decisions but on a steadfast commitment to his journey's purpose.

The Guardian appeared to Ray, reinforcing the importance of perseverance and staying on track. "In the face of tempting shortcuts, remember your grand vision," the Guardian advised. "Stay true to the path you have chosen, for greatness is not born of impatience but of enduring dedication."

With renewed determination, Ray resisted the temptations of the Taker of When. He embraced the idea of the long game, understanding that success was not an overnight achievement but a journey of growth and learning. The Guardian offered guidance on navigating challenges and finding opportunities for growth within setbacks.

Ray learned to adapt, pivot, and embrace challenges as stepping stones toward success. He no longer viewed setbacks as failures but as valuable lessons to propel him forward. Each obstacle presented an opportunity to refine his strategies and realign his actions with his vision.

As Ray confronted the Keepers of How and the Takers of When, he saw through their attempts to limit his potential. He realized that their job was to see if he could be distracted, and their tests were designed to prevent him from reaching his full potential if he allowed it. With the knowledge and wisdom gained from the Land of Where, Ray stood strong in the face of their challenges.

The Land of Where had become his fortress of resilience, and the future him whispered encouragement in his ear, reminding him of the audacious goals he had set for himself. Ray had come to understand that success was not just about reaching the destination but about the transformative journey he was undertaking.

In the face of adversity, Ray's emotional connection to his dreams grew even stronger. He embraced the challenges with a newfound sense of purpose, knowing that each test was an opportunity to prove his commitment to his vision.

The Land of Where had become his guide, and with each passing day, Ray became more determined to walk the path of greatness, staying true to the grand future he had envisioned for himself.

Chapter 9: Embracing Intention and Resilience

As Ray continued his sojourns in the Land of Where, the significance of intentional actions and thoughts became abundantly clear. The Guardian, always a guiding presence, emphasized the importance of consistency and discipline in shaping his future. Ray realized that his daily choices and behaviors held the key to aligning himself with his grand vision.

With each step forward, Ray encountered the Keeper of How and the Taker of When once again. This time, he faced them with newfound wisdom and emotional control, ready to confront their attempts to sway him from his path.

The Keeper of How tried to plant seeds of doubt in Ray's mind, questioning the feasibility of his audacious goals. But Ray was steadfast in his belief and refused to let doubt cloud his vision.

He understood that the path to greatness might be challenging, but he remained resolute in his pursuit.

Similarly, the Taker of When tempted Ray with shortcuts and instant gains, attempting to divert him from his long-term vision. However, Ray recognized the deceptive allure of quick fixes and instant success. He knew that true fulfillment and success required patience and perseverance.

With every test and challenge, Ray grew stronger and more confident in his ability to create the future he desired. He embraced adversities as opportunities for growth and learning, acknowledging that they were essential stepping stones on his journey to greatness.

The Guardian acknowledged Ray's resilience and determination, praising him for staying true to his purpose and remaining committed to his Where. Challenges were no longer perceived as obstacles but rather as valuable lessons that propelled him forward.

In the Land of Where, Ray learned that true success was not solely about achieving his goals; it was about the person he became along the way. The intentional actions and thoughts he cultivated each day were shaping his reality, bringing him closer to the future he envisioned.

Guided by the Guardian and inspired by his mentor James, Ray found strength in his journey. He understood that his path was unique, and comparisons to others were futile. Focused on his vision, Ray embraced every step with unwavering determination.

As days turned into weeks and weeks into months, Ray's confidence and belief in himself grew exponentially. Challenges would continue to arise, but he was now equipped with the tools to overcome them.

Returning to his everyday life, Ray carried the lessons from the Land of Where with him. Every decision, thought, and action he took contributed to the realization of his Where.

With intention as his guide and resilience as his armor, Ray faced the uncertainties of the future with unwavering courage. He had become the master of his fate, creating the reality he desired, and the world around him couldn't help but respond to the magnetic force of his determination.

Chapter 10: The Triumph of Transformation

As Ray continued his journey on the path to his "Where," he encountered obstacles and challenges that tested his resolve. However, with the guidance of the Guardian, he triumphed over these adversities and reaffirmed his commitment to his transformational journey.

The Guardian acknowledged Ray's growth and the tremendous strides he had taken since discovering the Land of Where. Ray had embraced his true purpose and had emerged as the best version of himself. His once mundane life as a janitor now sparkled with ambition and determination.

During one of his late-night conversations with Joseph, Ray learned the truth about the Land of Where. Joseph revealed that he, too, had experienced the mystical realm within the janitor's closet but chose not to disturb Ray's newfound growth by mentioning it.

Instead, he silently observed Ray's transformation, knowing that the Land of Where had a profound impact on his path to greatness.

Meanwhile, James noticed Ray's remarkable growth and saw the potential for even greater achievements. As a community leader, James introduced Ray to a new investment opportunity that aligned perfectly with his goals and vision. Ray's passion for entrepreneurship and investing found an outlet, and he eagerly embraced this new endeavor.

In the midst of his progress, the Keeper of How and the Taker of When approached Ray once more. This time, their demeanor was different; they commended Ray on his fortitude in the face of adversity. They acknowledged his ability to overcome their tests and offered sound advice on how to navigate the complexities of his entrepreneurial journey.

Ray was humbled by their acknowledgment and thanked them for their guidance. He had learned to recognize their role as testers of resolve, not adversaries. Their challenges had propelled him forward and made him stronger, enabling him to overcome his own self-doubt and limiting beliefs.

With each encounter, Ray's emotional connection to his dreams grew stronger. The Guardian's mystic concept of "the future you" leaving breadcrumbs on the path forward resonated deeply with him. Ray understood the significance of intentional actions and thoughts in shaping his destiny.

Consistency and discipline became his allies as he pursued his audacious goals. Ray embraced intentionality in his daily choices and behaviors, ensuring that they aligned with his grand vision of success.

He had come to realize that his emotions were powerful tools in manifesting his desired future. Both positive and negative emotions became valuable stepping stones on his transformative journey.

As Ray's self-belief strengthened, he summoned the courage to stand up to the Keeper of How and the Taker of When. Their negative influence could no longer sway him from his true path. The Guardian congratulated him on his growth and resilience, acknowledging his unwavering commitment to his dreams.

Ray's triumph over adversities, combined with his newfound emotional connection and intentional actions, led to a profound transformation. He had become a beacon of inspiration for others, proving that with dedication and perseverance, one could achieve greatness.

His journey continued, guided by the wisdom of the Guardian, the support of his friend Joseph, and the mentorship of James. The Land of Where remained his sacred sanctuary, the place where he connected with his true purpose and envisioned his grand future.

The road ahead was filled with opportunities and challenges, but Ray embraced each twist and turn with unwavering determination. With the Keeper of How and the Taker of When now by his side as allies, Ray moved forward with the knowledge that his journey was not just about reaching a destination but about becoming the person he was destined to be.

Chapter 11: Epilogue: The Everlasting Journey

Ray sat in his office, surrounded by the familiar sights and sounds of his newfound success. Time had passed since his last journey to the Land of Where, and life had taken on a vibrant new hue. As he gazed out the window, he couldn't help but reflect on the transformation he had experienced.

The memories of the Land of Where and the Guardian were etched in his mind. Those encounters had shaped his perspective and awakened a profound sense of purpose within him. The Land of Where had become more than just a mystical realm; it was a symbol of his ongoing pursuit of growth and fulfillment.

In the quiet moments, Ray cherished the wisdom imparted to him by the Guardian. The ethereal being had become a cherished mentor, guiding him on his journey of self-discovery and transformation.

The Land of Where held a special place in his heart, a reminder of the profound impact it had on his life.

As he sipped his coffee, Ray realized that his journey was far from over. Life's purpose was an ever-evolving adventure, and he was eager to continue exploring its vast landscape. The Keepers of How and Taker of When flickered in his thoughts, their tests and challenges forever etched in his memory.

Just as Ray's thoughts drifted, his phone rang, breaking the momentary silence. It was Joseph on the line, his voice tinged with urgency. Joseph mentioned the portal to the Land of Where, leaving Ray shocked and curious about what the call could mean.

As he listened to Joseph's words, Ray's heart raced with anticipation. The Land of Where had become a part of his life, and the prospect of revisiting its mystical realm filled him with excitement and trepidation.

In the corner of his eye, he noticed something peculiar—a flickering glow that seemed to dance in the air. It was The Flame of Why, the enigmatic presence that had briefly appeared in his life before, during one of his moments in the Land of Where. He didn't get to know The Flame of Why like The Guardian of Where, but he knew it was an important figure in the realm.

With a mix of uncertainty and determination, Ray knew that he couldn't ignore the call of the Land of Where and The Flame of Why. They held answers, challenges, and mysteries that awaited his discovery.

As he stood up from his desk, Ray felt a surge of energy. The office that had once been mundane now held the promise of infinite possibilities. The Land of Where had given him the tools to shape his destiny, and he was ready to embrace whatever lay ahead.

With a final glance at his office, he stepped into the unknown. The everlasting journey of self-discovery and growth continued, with the Land of Where, as his guiding light, The Guardian as his mentor, and The Flame of Why as a constant enigmatic presence.

And so, with his heart brimming with curiosity and his spirit alight with purpose, Ray embarked on the next chapter of his extraordinary journey, eager to embrace the mysteries that lay before him.

Notes

Notes

Notes

Notes

<u>Notes</u>

About the Author

Hey there, I'm Chris, and I've been on an entrepreneurial adventure for the past 10 years. It all began when I decided to take a leap of faith and quit a good job to pursue my passion for entrepreneurship. Little did I know that this journey would lead me down a path of creating not one, but two successful service-oriented companies that generated six-figure revenues.

To be honest, my original intention for starting my own "business" was to fund my rap career, but life had different plans for me. Over the years, I've come to realize that failure has been my greatest teacher. I've failed forward time and time again, and that process hasn't always been glamorous. Looking back, I'd give some sage advice to my 29-year-old self.

Yet, despite the setbacks, my failures fueled my hunger for knowledge. I've accumulated an Audible collection of over 400 audiobooks, transforming my experiences into new opportunities. From my failures, I grew into a business consultant and tax specialist, and even published my 1st book. Not to mention, I built the successful "Business of Hair and Beauty" brand and became a respected barber instructor.

But more than just personal achievements, my failures have taught me something invaluable – that every stumble is a chance to learn and grow. Now, my burning desire is to motivate, inspire, and educate fellow entrepreneurs. I want to empower them on their journey, helping them uncover their "Where," embrace their "Why," and equip them with the tools to execute their "What" and live their best lives, right now.

My mission is to make a positive impact by sharing my experiences and guiding others through the challenges of entrepreneurship with resilience and determination. Together, let's learn from our failures and pave the way to success.

www.ingramcontent.com/pod-product-compliance
Lightning Source LLC
Chambersburg PA
CBHW062252290526
45794CB00006B/2515